Slap-Shot Science!

by
Ben Grossblatt
and Paul Beck

Welcome to the Lab!
To start assembling your
Air Hockey table right away,
turn to page 24!

W9-CTB-986

Slap-Shot Science!

Published by SmartLab®, an imprint of becker&mayer!
All rights reserved. ArtLab® and SmartLab® are registered trademarks of becker&mayer! LLC, 11120 NE 33rd Place, Suite 101, Bellevue, Washington.
Creative development by Jim Becker and Anna Johnson

If you have questions or comments about this product, please visit www.smartlabtoys.com/customerservice.html and click on the Customer Service Request Form.

Edited by Betsy Pringle
Written by Ben Grossblatt and Paul Beck
Designed by Andrew Hess
Illustrated by Damon Brown
Assembly illustrations by Ryan Hobson
Image research by Zena Chew
SmartLab® character and product photography by Keith Megay
Product development by Mark Byrnes, Christine Lee, and Chris Tanner
Production management by Larry Weiner
Project management by Beth Lenz

Image credits: Page 8: Indonesian air train © William Pemberton; page 9: child in wind tunnel, image from SkyVenture Arizona; page 10: hovercraft, image from Craftima Oy, Finland; page 11: air bearing floor, image from NASA; page 21: air-hockey playing robot, image from Mark W. Spong, Coordinated Science Lab, University of Illinois at Urbana-Champaign.

Printed, manufactured, and assembled in China.

Slap-Shot Science! is part of the SmartLab® Face-Off Air Hockey kit. Not to be sold separately.

10 9 8 7 6 5 4 3 2 1

ISBN-10: 1-60380-003-4
ISBN-13: 978-1-60380-003-7
07098

AIR HOCKEY

Air hockey requires physical and mental toughness and nerves of steel! Although you might think of it as nothing more than a fast, fun way to compete, there is actually a lot going on beneath air hockey's entertaining surface.

It combines air and hockey. Sounds simple enough. (Wait, it gets better.) You see, air is powerful stuff. And there's a lot of science hidden in that floating puck.

In this book, you'll find out all about air hockey science. First, you'll learn about air—what it's made of and where it gets its mighty power. Next, it's on to the physics of falling apples, bouncing balls, and speeding pucks. Then you'll get a quick air hockey clinic, where you'll learn the shots and strategies of the game.

Finally, you'll assemble your own mini air hockey table, so you can see firsthand what it's all about.

First stop: Air.

Air hockey. It's been called the Sport of Kings. Plaything of Heroes. Fury on a Tabletop. (Of course, it's only been called those things by the authors of this book.)

SAY HELLO TO AIR

Open a window and take a look at some air around you. What do you see? Unless you're in the middle of a smog alert, you don't see anything. Air is invisible. And tasteless. And odorless. So it's a whole lot of nothing, right? Wrong.

Air is a soup of different gases—an invisible soup that doesn't taste like anything. Nitrogen and oxygen are the main ingredients. There's also a dash of argon, a pinch of carbon dioxide, and a tiny seasoning of neon, helium, methane, krypton, hydrogen, and xenon (ZEE-non). But for air hockey and the other uses of air power in this book, the particular mix doesn't matter. You can think of the whole mix as a single gas.

Gas is one of the five states of matter. Matter is anything that is made of atoms and molecules.

INGREDIENTS: OXYGEN, NEON, NITROGEN, ARGON, HELIUM, KRYPTON, XENON

What's the Matter?

Besides gases, the other states of matter are solids, liquids, plasmas, and a new one called Bose-Einstein condensates. For air hockey purposes, we'll stick to the basic three: solids, liquids, and gases. The different states of matter depend on the strength of the force between molecules.

Solid: molecules are bound tightly together.

Liquid: forces between molecules are weaker than in a solid.

Gas: forces between molecules are very weak.

In a gas, unlike in a liquid or solid, the molecules are free to move around wherever they can go. And move they do. A gas will keep on expanding, the molecules moving farther and farther apart, until something stops it. If it's in a container, the gas expands to fill the whole container. On Earth, it's the planet's gravity that keeps the air in place.

Hooray for Air!

Even when it's not "doing" anything, air is a crucial part of your life. For one thing, we all need it to breathe. If there's no air, there's no breathing. And if there's no breathing, there's no living. Also, some of the gases in the air-soup mix keep life livable by trapping some of the sun's energy, while reflecting back the rest. Without air, the earth would be a furnace during the day and a deep-freeze at night.

But when air starts moving, things really get interesting. Air in motion is powerful stuff, whether it's the destructive power of a hurricane or tornado, the useful power of a wind generator, or the powerful fun of air hockey.

THE PRESSURE'S ON!

Air is invisible, but there are things about it that you can measure. You can measure the temperature. You can measure its volume, or the amount of space it takes up. And most importantly for air hockey, you can measure the pressure.

Pressure is the pushing force of the air. On the surface of the earth, it's the weight of all the air pressing down. In a container like a tank or balloon, it's the force of the moving air molecules bouncing off the inside of the container. Pressure force is always measured over a particular amount of surface area, such as pounds per square inch.

You might not know it, but you're under a lot of pressure yourself, right now. That's because there's a pile of air on top of your head going all the way up to the edge of space. It doesn't look like much—you can see all the way through it, after all—but the weight of all those molecules adds up. At sea level, the air presses down with an average force of more than 14 pounds per square inch. That means the stack of air on top of your head weighs more than 400 pounds!

400lbs

Blowin' in the Wind

Earth's atmosphere isn't an even layer of air over the whole planet. It's bumpy, uneven, and moving all the time. It gets pushed, stretched, and piled up over different spots. Depending on where the sun is and what's on the ground (or water), different areas of the atmosphere absorb different amounts of heat. Hot air expands and gets less dense. Cool air contracts and gets denser.

All of this creates differences in air pressure between different areas of the planet. When there's a pressure difference, the air moves. It always goes from the place where the pressure is higher to a place where the pressure is lower. When that happens in the atmosphere it means one thing: wind!

Far Out!

How high does the air go? There's no exact answer. The atmosphere doesn't have a sharp border. It just gets less and less dense the farther up you go. If you could fly to a height of 19 miles, you'd be above 99% of the air. At a height of 60 miles, you'd officially be in space. But there would still be far-apart air molecules all around you.

AIR FORCE

When air is moving, anything in the way gets pushed. If it's a gentle breeze, it ruffles your hair. If it's a hurricane, it can blow your house down!

People figured out a long time ago that they could harness wind power to get things done. Put a sail on your boat, and presto! No more strenuous paddling. Build a windmill, and you can turn the pushing power of wind into spinning power to grind your grain or pump water from your well.

Now, that old-fashioned wind technology has been updated in high-tech ways. Racing sailboats set records with sails made of Kevlar, the same material used in bulletproof vests. Wind farms with rows of spinning turbines generate electricity without pollution. These modern windmills can be truly gigantic. Each of the fiberglass blades on the world's largest wind turbine is longer than half a football field!

Sailtrain

An air-propelled train in Jakarta, Indonesia, uses the power of air to zip along its track. Blowers get the air moving along a duct inside the track, where it pushes against an air-catching plate attached to the train chassis above. The train rolls on wheels with air-powered ease.

Even the air train isn't a new idea. In 1870, an inventor named Alfred Ely Beach built an air-powered subway under the streets of New York City. A gigantic blower forced air into the tunnel, pushing the train along. When it was time to go the other way, the blower was reversed, and the train was sucked backward.

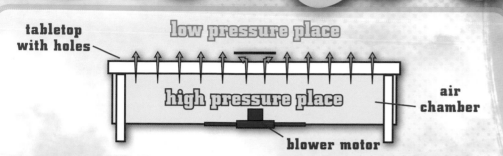

tabletop with holes

low pressure place

high pressure place

air chamber

blower motor

So what does all this wind stuff have do with air hockey? Easy! It's all about air moving from a high pressure place to a low pressure place. The motor and fan in your air hockey table get the air moving and build up pressure inside. The only way for the high-pressure air inside the table to get to the lower-pressure area outside is through the tiny holes in the tabletop. The power of the air flowing out of the holes is enough to lift the plastic puck right off the surface!

Want to turn yourself into a human air hockey puck? You can do it in a vertical wind tunnel. The tunnel's fans pack winds of more than 100 miles per hour, rushing straight up. That's enough air power to keep even a large adult flying. Skydivers use the tunnels for training, but lots of people take flight just for fun.

TURNING THINGS UPSIDE DOWN

An air hockey puck rides on high-pressure air flowing up from the table. But what if the air flowed down from the bottom of the puck instead? That's the idea behind a hovercraft. A hovercraft is a vehicle that rides on a cushion of air. Because it has no wheels, a hovercraft can travel on both water and land. Hovercraft come in all sizes, from single-seaters to gigantic ferries that carry hundreds of passengers.

A hovercraft gets its hover from one or more fans that blow air downward under the craft's platform. A flexible skirt around the platform creates a chamber to trap the air underneath. As the chamber fills, the hovercraft rises on the cushion of trapped air. Propellers and rudders on top push and steer the craft.

Moving Made Easy

Air bearings, or air casters, are like mini-hovercraft for moving heavy loads. When the air bearing is hooked up to a compressor, air flows out of the bottom to create a layer of high-pressure air that lifts the bearing and its load. The heavy load glides on a cushion of air about as thick as one of your hairs.

With air bearings, people can levitate massive objects with ease. How massive? Try 1,700 tons! That's the weight of the movable seating sections in Honolulu's Aloha Stadium. The banks of seats glide on air bearings as they're moved into place for different sports.

Air bearings are also used for shifting gigantic stage sets, satellites, and rocket and aircraft parts. And because air bearings let huge objects glide with weightless ease, NASA astronauts use them to train for moving heavy loads in space.

Try This!
Make A Hovercraft!

Make your own hovercraft with a paper cup, a drinking straw, a rubber band, and a balloon.

1. Cut a straw-sized hole in the bottom of the cup.
2. Cut the straw so it is about 1" longer than the cup.
3. Place the balloon on one end of the straw and wrap a rubber band around the balloon's neck to hold it on.
4. Blow into the straw to blow up the balloon.
5. Pinching the neck of the inflated balloon, push the open end of the straw into the cup and set the cup on a smooth surface.
6. Release the balloon. The air in the balloon will lift the cup and make it move!

THE PUCK DOESN'T STOP HERE

What would air hockey be like without the air? Mighty slow, that's what. With no cushion of air to glide on, the puck would scrape to a halt before it got very far. But with air power, the puck never stops.

Newton's First Law of Motion

"An object at rest will tend to stay at rest, and an object in motion will tend to stay in motion (in a straight line) unless acted upon by an outside force."

The science behind air hockey's nonstop puck goes back to Sir Isaac Newton, the English mathematician and physicist. More than 300 years ago, Newton came up with rules describing the way everything in the universe moves, called Newton's Laws of Motion. There were three of them, but the first—known, naturally enough, as "Newton's First Law of Motion"—is the one with the most to tell us about air hockey.

If a puck is sliding across the air hockey table, Newton's First Law tells us that it'll keep sliding in the same direction forever—unless some force gets into the act.

Newton's Noggin

When people like Isaac Newton talk about a force, they mean the pressure or the action that makes an object do something. You already know about the force of gravity. That's the force that makes a plate of spaghetti go splat on the floor when you push it off the table. (Why'd you do that?) You have probably also noticed the push and pull of magnets when you place them close together. That's called magnetic force.

In air hockey, the force that affects your sliding puck could be your opponent's paddle, or it could be *friction*. Friction is the force that slows things down when they move over a surface. Friction happens whenever two things rub against each other. The surfaces might look smooth to your unaided eye, but under a microscope you'd see that they're actually covered with tiny bumps and ridges. The rougher the surface and object are, the more spots there are to rub against each other and slow the movement down.

Hockey puck, magnified 400 times

Sir Isaac Newton (1642-1727) is considered one of the foremost scientific thinkers of all time. According to legend, Newton started thinking about motion after he got smacked on the head by a falling air hockey puck. Okay, it was actually an apple. And fine, the story probably isn't even really true. But it's a good story!

FRICTION
IN ACTION...AND OUT OF ACTION!

Try This!

1. Take two paperback books that are the same size.
2. Tightly "gift wrap" one of the books in a paper towel.
3. Holding a baking sheet or a smooth board at an angle, let each book slide down the ramp.

The book covered with the rough paper towel will slide more slowly because there are more rough places on the towel to grip the board or baking sheet.
Try it!

Speedy games like air hockey (and its cousin, ice hockey) are all about minimizing friction. In ice hockey, the puck and players zip around on slippery ice. In air hockey, there's a layer of air between the puck and the table. The puck has nothing to rub against but air, so friction is out of the action.

Reducing friction by putting a layer of something slippery in between two rubbing surfaces is called *lubrication*. The slippery stuff is called a *lubricant*. Oil and grease are common lubricants, used in cars, bikes, and just about every other kind of machine with moving parts. There are also dry lubricants, such as graphite—a powdered version of the same material that pencil "lead" is made of.

Air hockey uses plain old ordinary air as a lubricant. Good thing, too! Oil hockey would be a messy, messy game.

Sources of Forces

According to Newton's First Law of Motion, an air hockey puck will keep moving in a straight line unless a force acts on it. (Or keep standing still if it's standing still—but when is an air hockey puck ever standing still?) In an air hockey game, the puck zips around all over the place, changing speed and direction all the time. With friction mostly out of the picture, there must be other forces in on the action, right? Right.

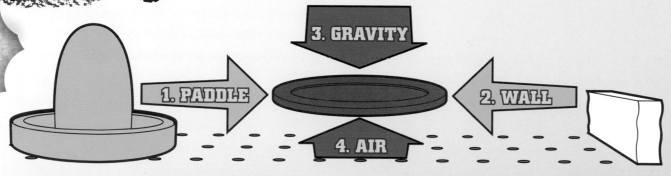

3. GRAVITY

1. PADDLE

2. WALL

4. AIR

1. There's force from you and your paddle. It's what sends the puck shooting off toward your opponent's goal. If the puck happens to be standing still, it's also the force that gets the puck moving.

2. There's force from the table's walls. When the puck hits a wall, the wall pushes back—hard enough to send the puck off in another direction.

3. There's force from Earth. Gravity keeps the puck on the table.

4. There's force from the cushion of air under the puck. It's exactly enough to balance against gravity and keep the puck suspended.

TOTALLY ANGULAR

Knowing that the puck will travel in a straight line can help you play better air hockey.

Try This!

When an object bounces off a surface, you can predict where it will end up. How? By knowing that the angle of reflection equals the angle of incidence. (Oh, sure, that's good and clear!) In other words, the puck will bounce off the wall at the same angle that it hit the wall. When your puck hits the wall, it won't stop, go in a circle, or bounce off at some random angle.

This principle lets you know where to aim your banking shots in air hockey (or in billiards, for that matter). It also tells you where your paddle needs to be to block your opponent's shots.

Angle of incidence (hit)   43°   43°   Angle of reflection (bounce)

1. Sit on the floor, facing a wall about five or six feet away.
2. Roll a ball—a tennis ball works great—toward the wall and see what happens after it hits.

If you roll it at the wall directly in front of you, it'll bounce right back to you. But if you roll it toward the wall at an angle, it'll bounce away from you at the same angle. Try it!

AIR HOCKEY

The real wonder of air hockey is that all that science and air power, all the principles of the hovercraft and Sir Isaac Newton, can fit on a tiny table.

An air hockey table resembles a miniature ice hockey rink but, instead of ice, the surface is covered with tiny holes. Blowers pump air out through the holes, and that creates a layer of air for the puck to glide on.

The game consists of a table, a puck, and two paddles. The paddles are also called mallets or strikers.

The object is to shoot the puck into your opponent's goal. You can hit the puck wherever you want—right at the goal or banked off the wall—but you can't hit it at all if it's on your opponent's side of the table.

The blower inside the table forces air through the holes on the top. As the puck glides over the holes, the air is pressed down and out in all directions. This creates a cushion of air under the puck.

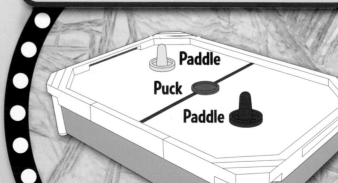

Paddle

Puck

Paddle

APPLYING PHYSICS TO HOCKEY

When an object strikes a hard surface at an angle, it bounces off at the same angle. If you couldn't count on this little principle of physics, the only way you could score points would be to aim the puck directly at the goal. And what kind of fun would that be?

Banking shot

Banking shots—where the puck bounces off a wall and into the goal—add excitement and challenge to the game. With practice, you'll get a feel for where to aim the puck and how to make those clutch shots. It's all in the angles.

The Shots

Straight shot

The simplest shot is called a straight. In a straight, you shoot the puck straight for the goal. Nothing flashy, but it has its place.

Unders

Unders are banking shots (where the puck bounces off the wall). You shoot an under between your opponent's paddle and the goal.

Cut shot

A cut shot is a little trickier. When you shoot a cut, you slide the paddle to one side, toward the puck. When you reach the puck, you flick the paddle against it, so that the puck goes in the other direction. Well executed, this shot is sure to surprise your opponent.

Overs

Overs are similar to unders. That's why they work so well. When your opponent sets up to defend against an under, you change the shot and launch an over: the puck travels in front of your opponent's paddle and sails into the goal.

Air Hockey Tricks

To bump your game up a notch, master the moves called drifts. With drifts, you get your opponent off guard by keeping the puck in motion on your side of the table. That way, it's hard to predict where the shot will come from.

Side-to-side drift

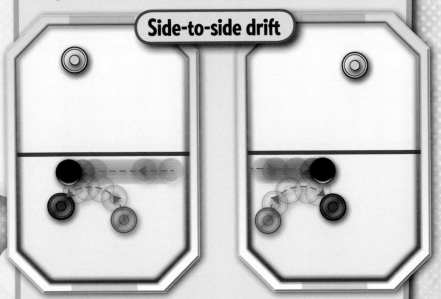

To perform a side-to-side drift, hit the puck from one wall to the other. After the puck bounces against the wall and then slides across the table and bounces off the other wall, hit it again to keep this back-and-forth, wall-to-wall movement going. When will you decide to shoot? No one knows but you.

A combo is a puck position that gives you two possible shots. This doubles your chances for scoring. Take a look at this combo to get an idea of the possibilities.

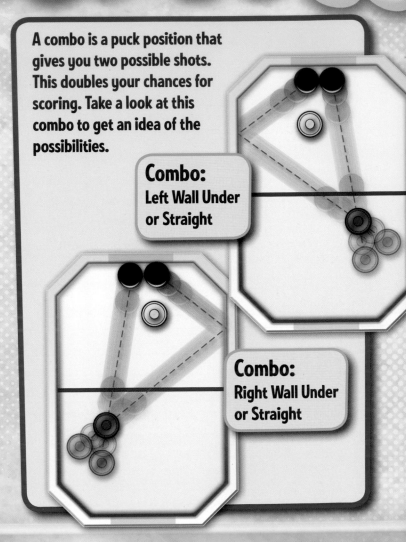

Combo:
Left Wall Under or Straight

Combo:
Right Wall Under or Straight

These are just some of the tactics that can sharpen your air hockey skills. Invent more as you play. (Feel free to name your new moves after yourself.)

Practice Makes Perfect

Hockey Bot

A great way to sharpen your shots—aside from trying them over and over—is to practice them wrong-handed. If you're right-handed, try making some straights or banking shots left-handed. (And vice versa if you're a lefty.) You'd be surprised how well this can improve your sense of distances on the table, as well as how to hit those bank shots.

> Practice scoring goals by sending the puck around and between small obstacles.

A similar skill-enhancement technique is eyes-closed shooting. Think you can do it? Can you make a full-table cut at the goal? Can you judge the angles with your eyes closed? Keep at it and maybe you'll be able to play by sound alone. (Only the finest players in the world can play by smell.)

Students at several colleges are hard at work building air-hockey-playing robots. The robots not only have to block shots, they must also try to score goals. This means the robots have to be able to predict the action of the puck. (Newton's First Law would help them do that, right?) Students believe their air-hockey-playing robots will help scientists develop robots that can perform jobs that are too dangerous for people to do, such as exploring volcanoes.

21

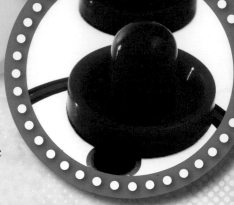

SET A RECORD

If you want to track your progress, keep a record of your personal bests. This is how athletes often push themselves. They like to think they're mostly competing against themselves. Very philosophical.

To chart your personal bests, try your hand at these events. Write down your best scores and keep checking back to see how much better you're getting!

End-to-End (strength)

How many times can you make the puck bounce off one end of the table and then the other, with one shot?

Targets (accuracy)

Put a moving target on the table. (A ping-pong ball works well, and so does a wind-up walking toy.) How many times in a row can you hit it?

Zigzag (finesse)

How many banks in a row can you make while scoring a goal? Can you make the puck zig off one wall and then zag off the other and into the goal? How many zigs and zags can you achieve with one shot?

One-Minute Warning (speed)

How many shots of any kind can you send into the goal in only one minute?

Air Hockey RULES!

- Flip a coin to see who starts the game.
- Each goal is worth one point.
- When the puck contacts any part of the centerline, either player may strike the puck.
- After a point is scored, the player scored upon gets the puck.
- All fouls result in the opponent gaining possession of the puck.

FOULS

- Completely crossing the centerline with the paddle onto the other player's side of the table
- Hitting the puck off the table
- Placing the paddle on top of the puck

Official rules say you play to seven points. But who says you need to be official? Play as long or as short a game as you want. And why not dream up your own rules, while you're at it?

Congratulations!

Now you understand the power of air, the science of hockey, and the majesty that is air hockey.

Time to put it all into play and get assembling, get practicing, and get winning.

The instructions that follow will guide you through the assembly steps, and before you know it, you'll be the proud owner of a working air hockey table!

PARTS

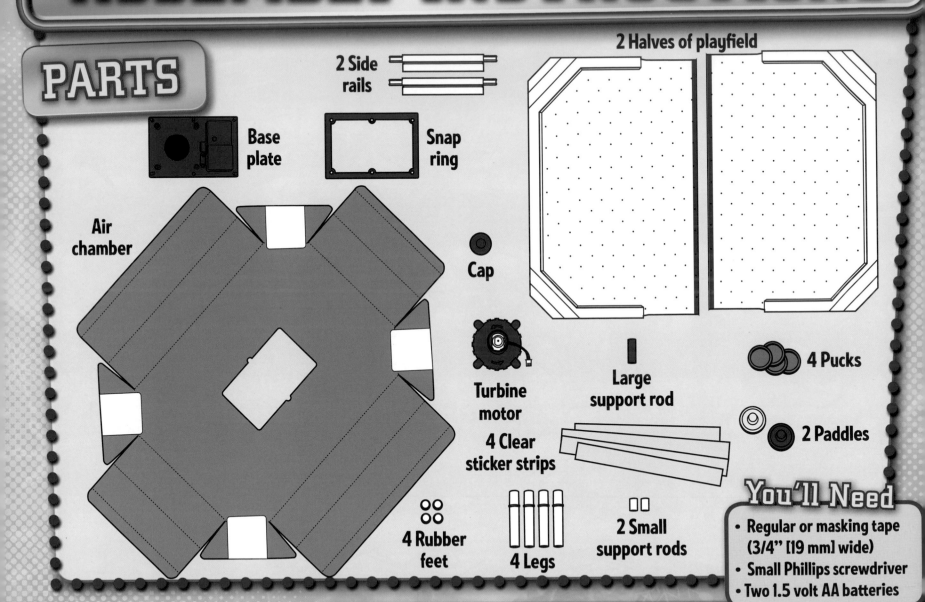

2 Side rails

Base plate

Snap ring

2 Halves of playfield

Air chamber

Cap

Turbine motor

Large support rod

4 Pucks

4 Clear sticker strips

2 Paddles

4 Rubber feet

4 Legs

2 Small support rods

You'll Need

- Regular or masking tape (3/4" [19 mm] wide)
- Small Phillips screwdriver
- Two 1.5 volt AA batteries

Before You Begin

Hold the turbine with the fan pointing toward the floor. Flick the fan with your finger to make sure it spins freely. If it drags, gently pull the fan a tiny bit away from the housing, so it does not touch.

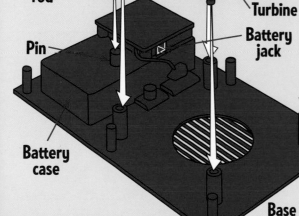

Cap

Battery plug

Motor

Pin

Large support rod

Turbine

Pin

Battery jack

Post

Battery case

Base plate

1 Place the cap on the motor.

2 Insert the battery plug into the battery jack (it only fits one way).

3 Press the four pins on the turbine into the four posts on the base plate.

4 One end of the large support rod has a smaller hole. Press the end with the small hole onto the pin on the battery case.

Assembled turbine

This is so simple, even a pup can do it!

1 Turn over the turbine and remove the screw from the battery case.

2 Insert two 1.5 volt AA batteries into the case, following the diagram inside the battery case. Screw the back onto the case.

3 Keeping your fingers and all objects away from the fan, move the switch to the "on" position.
Turn off the fan.

If the fan does not work, check that the battery plug is pushed in all the way, and that the batteries are fresh and are inserted with the correct polarity.

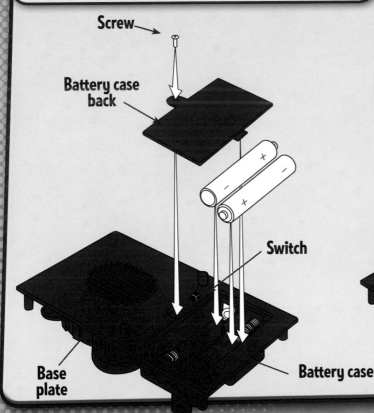

Screw

Battery case back

Switch

Base plate

Battery case

- To ensure proper safety and operation, the battery replacement must always be done by an adult.
- Never let a child use this product unless the battery door is secure.
- Keep all batteries away from small children, and immediately dispose of any exhausted batteries safely.
- Batteries are small objects and could be ingested.
- Do not recharge nonrechargeable batteries.
- Remove rechargeable batteries from the toy before charging them.
- Rechargeable batteries are only to be charged under adult supervision.
- Different types of batteries or new and used batteries are not to be mixed.
- Only use batteries of the same or equivalent types as recommended.
- Do not mix alkaline, standard (carbon-zinc), or rechargeable (nickel-cadmium) batteries.
- Insert batteries with the correct polarity.
- Remove exhausted batteries from the toy.
- Do not short-circuit the supply terminals.

Air Chamber

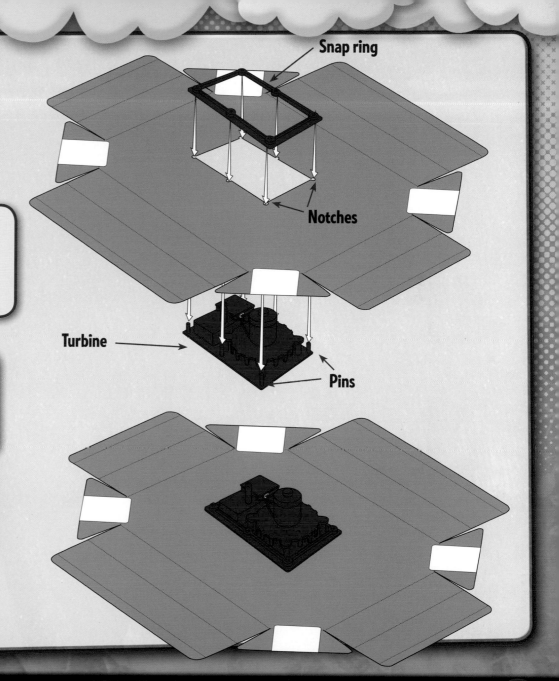

Snap ring

Notches

Turbine

Pins

1 Unfold the air chamber and place it, plain side up, over the turbine. The six notches in the air chamber will match the pins on the base plate.

2 With the smooth, flat side of the snap ring facing DOWN, place the snap ring over the six pins on the base plate.

3 Pushing from the other side, press each pin securely through the holes on the snap ring to get a snug, airtight fit.

1. Bend the corner pieces toward the inside of the chamber.

2. Bend all the tabs toward the center.

3. Fold the end pieces over tabs A and B. Make sure the brown part of each tab is completely tucked under the folded end.

4. Use your own masking or regular tape to tape the folded end to the floor of the air chamber.

Fold up and tape the ends and corners

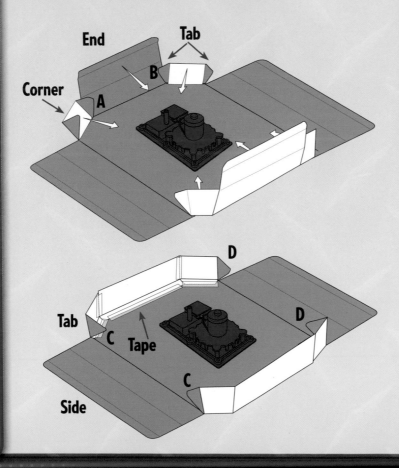

End **Tab** **Corner** **A** **B**

Tab **C** **Tape** **D** **D** **C** **Side**

1. Fold the side pieces over tabs C and D. Make sure the brown part of each tab is completely tucked under the folded side.

2. Use your own masking or regular tape to tape the folded side to the floor of the air chamber.

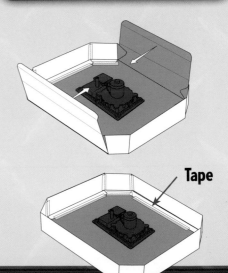

Tape

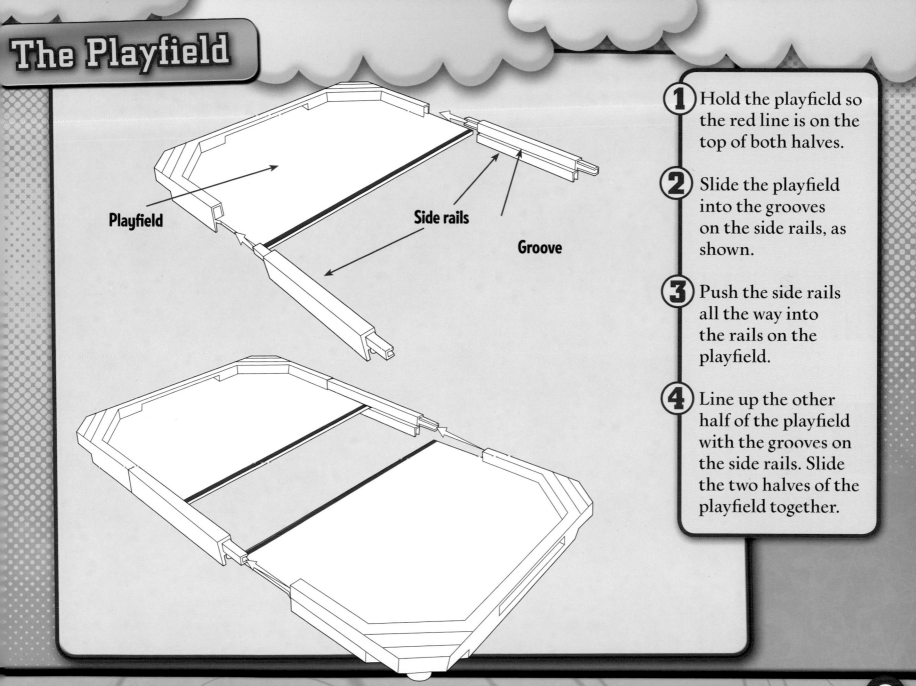

Playfield

Side rails

Groove

1 Hold the playfield so the red line is on the top of both halves.

2 Slide the playfield into the grooves on the side rails, as shown.

3 Push the side rails all the way into the rails on the playfield.

4 Line up the other half of the playfield with the grooves on the side rails. Slide the two halves of the playfield together.

Attaching the Air Chamber to the Playfield

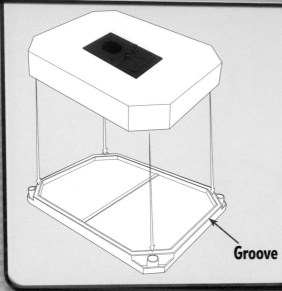

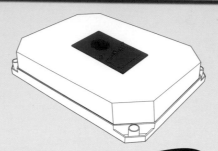

Groove

(1) Lay the playfield upside down on a flat surface. Position the air chamber over the playfield, as shown.

(2) Carefully press the air chamber into the groove around the edge of the playfield.

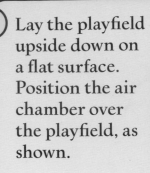

> When all of the edges are inside the groove, press down firmly with both hands to secure the air chamber to the playfield.

Sealing the Air Chamber

To completely seal the air chamber, use the clear sticker strips provided in your kit to tape the air chamber to the plastic playfield. Cover part of the cardboard and part of the plastic as you seal around the edges.

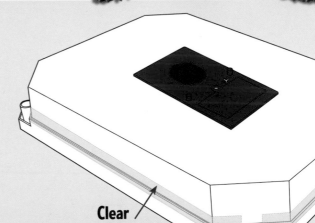

Clear sticker strip

Clear sticker strip

Legs

1. Insert the four legs into the posts on the playfield.

2. Press a rubber foot into each post.

3. Place the narrow ends of the two base plate support rods over the pins in the base plate.

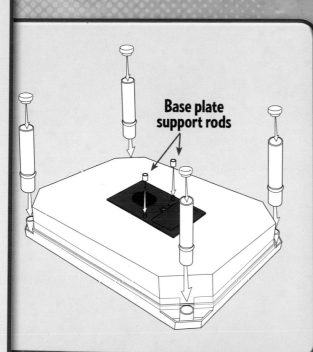

Base plate support rods

Turn over the assembled air hockey table. Lay a puck on the table and turn on the motor.

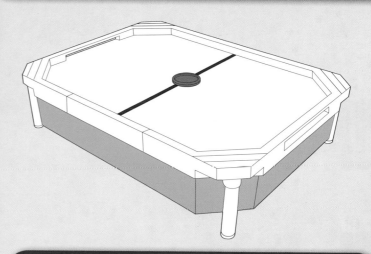

If your puck doesn't lightly float when you turn on the motor, check to make sure there aren't any gaps where air is leaking:

- Make sure the two halves of the playfield are pressed tightly together.
- Tape all the places where the air chamber meets the plastic pieces, including around the turbine on the bottom.
- Tape the corners of the air chamber.

Scoreboard assembly

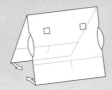

1 Fold the top along the fold line.

2 Fold up the two bottom pieces so they are inside the front and back of the scoreboard.

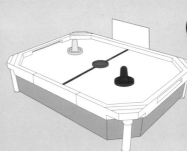

3 Flatten the scoreboard and tape it to the side of your air hockey table.

Freestanding Scoreboard

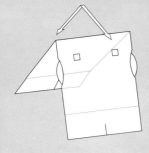

1 Fold the top along the fold line.

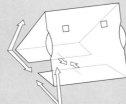

2 Fold the two bottom pieces toward the center, so the scoreboard looks like a triangle.

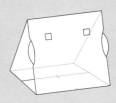

3 Interlock the bottom pieces at the cut lines.

Now get outta here and go make air hockey history!

32